y
MW01381279

# THIS BOOK BELONGS TO

_____

# STONE MOSAIC. BOOK 3.

## Stress-free color by number book.

Try this stress-free color by number book by coloring different stone shapes to reveal the picture.
It's the 3d book from this series.

Big and small circles and ovals colored in the same 22-colors palette as in all other our books will make the process of coloring relaxing and the result colorful and bright.

**Enjoy this new series of color by number books!**

# TRY YOUR PALETTE

1. Peach
2. Yellow
3. Skin Tone
4. Orange
5. Orangered
6. Red Brown
7. Brown
8. Dark Brown
9. Pink
10. Scarlet
11. Red
12. Lilac
13. Violet
14. Light Blue
15. Blue
16. Dark Blue
17. Light Green
18. Green
19. Dark Green
20. Gray
21. Dark Gray
22. Black

1. Peach
2. Yellow
3. Skin Tone
4. Orange
5. Orangered
6. Red Brown
7. Brown
8. Dark Brown
9. Pink
10. Scarlet
11. Red
12. Lilac
13. Violet
14. Light Blue
15. Blue
16. Dark Blue
17. Light Green
18. Green
19. Dark Green
20. Gray
21. Dark Gray
22. Black

| | | | | |
|---|---|---|---|---|
| 1 | Peach | 12 | Lilac |
| 2 | Yellow | 13 | Violet |
| 3 | Skin Tone | 14 | Light Blue |
| 4 | Orange | 15 | Blue |
| 5 | Orangered | 16 | Dark Blue |
| 6 | Red Brown | 17 | Light Green |
| 7 | Brown | 18 | Green |
| 8 | Dark Brown | 19 | Dark Green |
| 9 | Pink | 20 | Gray |
| 10 | Scarlet | 21 | Dark Gray |
| 11 | Red | 22 | Black |

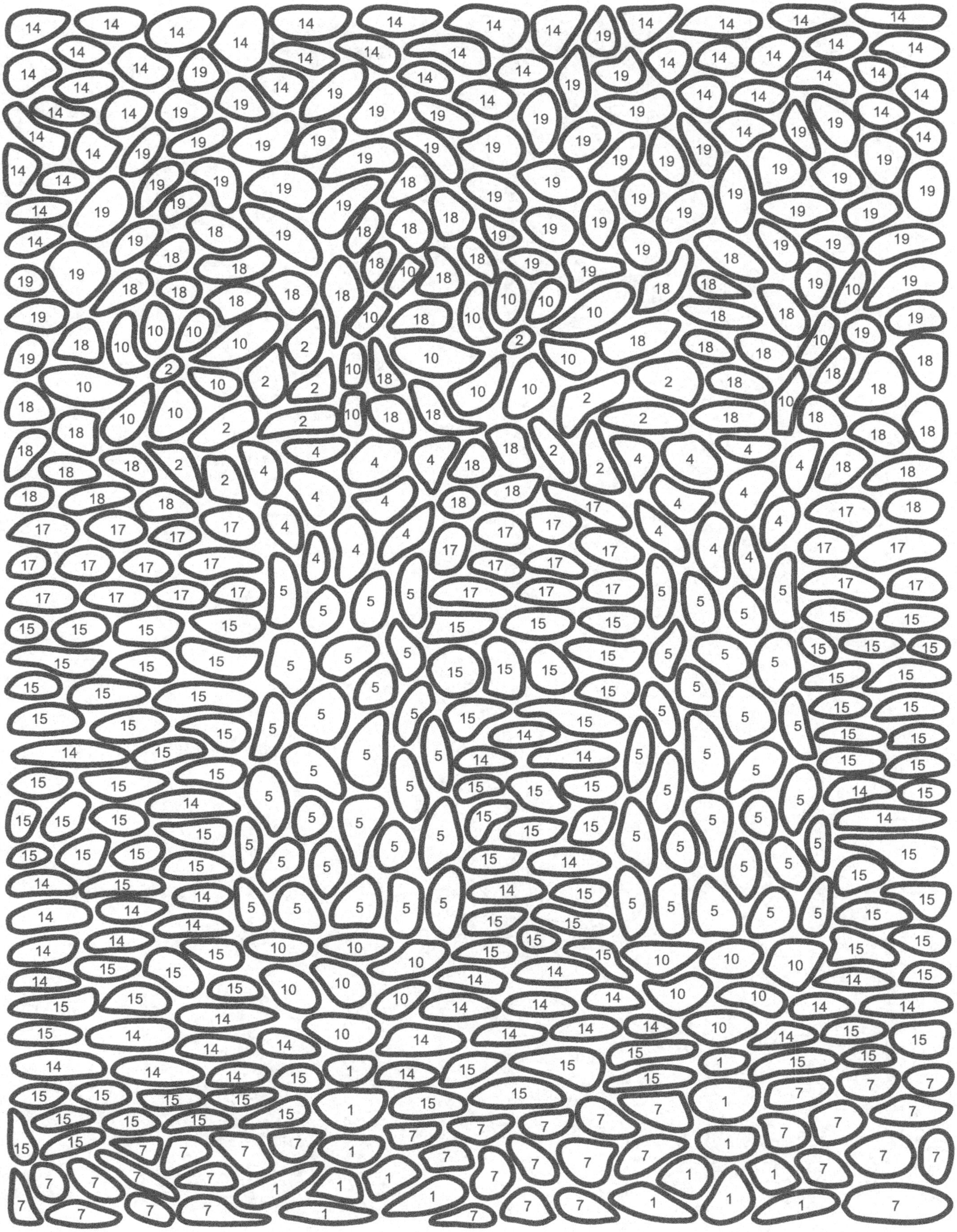

| | | | | | |
|---|---|---|---|---|---|
| 1 | Peach | 9 | Pink | 17 | Light Green |
| 2 | Yellow | 10 | Scarlet | 18 | Green |
| 3 | Skin Tone | 11 | Red | 19 | Dark Green |
| 4 | Orange | 12 | Lilac | 20 | Gray |
| 5 | Orangered | 13 | Violet | 21 | Dark Gray |
| 6 | Red Brown | 14 | Light Blue | 22 | Black |
| 7 | Brown | 15 | Blue | | |
| 8 | Dark Brown | 16 | Dark Blue | | |

| 1 | Peach | 9 | Pink | 17 | Light Green |
| 2 | Yellow | 10 | Scarlet | 18 | Green |
| 3 | Skin Tone | 11 | Red | 19 | Dark Green |
| 4 | Orange | 12 | Lilac | 20 | Gray |
| 5 | Orangered | 13 | Violet | 21 | Dark Gray |
| 6 | Red Brown | 14 | Light Blue | 22 | Black |
| 7 | Brown | 15 | Blue | | |
| 8 | Dark Brown | 16 | Dark Blue | | |

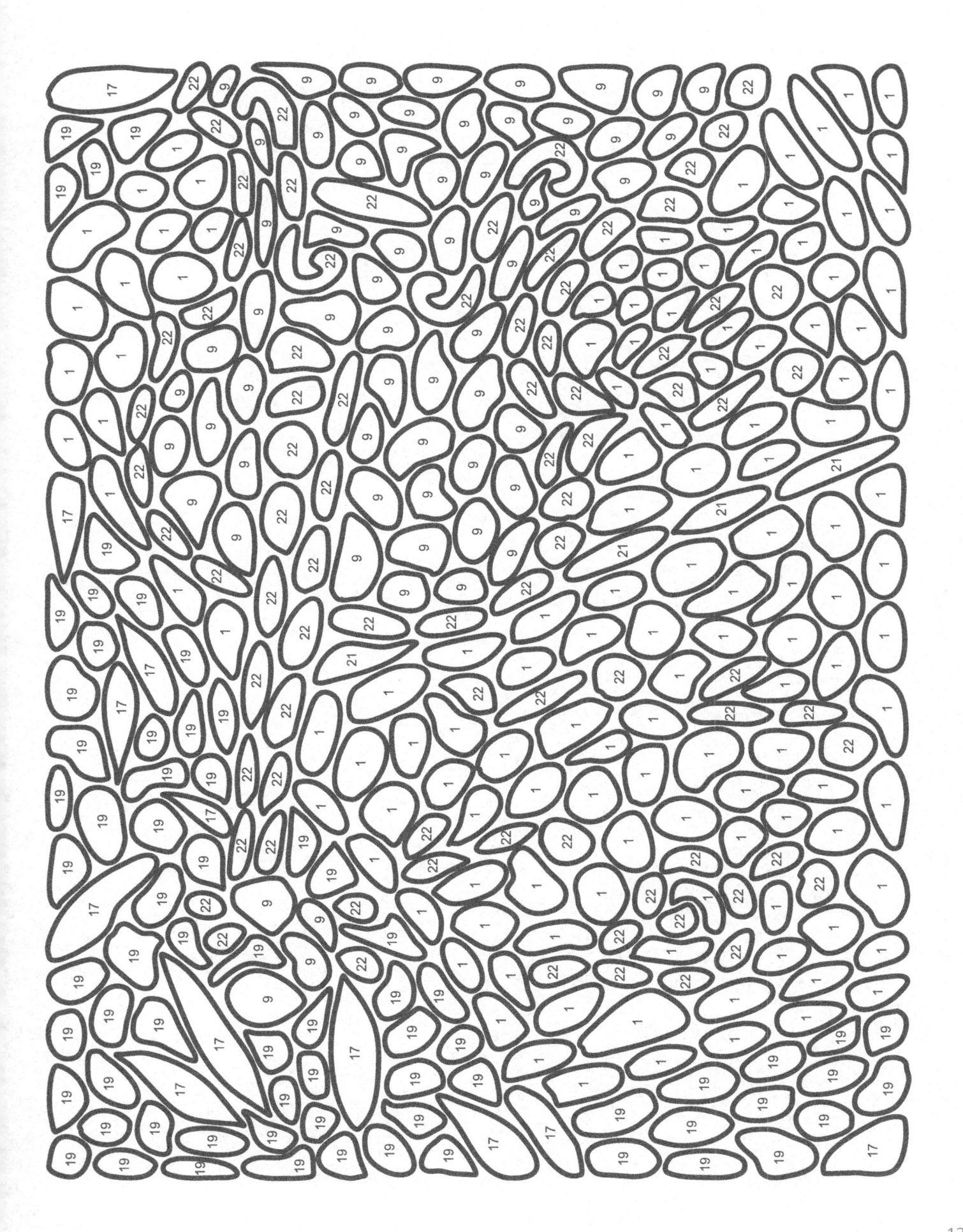

| | | | | |
|---|---|---|---|---|
| 1 | Peach | 12 | Lilac |
| 2 | Yellow | 13 | Violet |
| 3 | Skin Tone | 14 | Light Blue |
| 4 | Orange | 15 | Blue |
| 5 | Orangered | 16 | Dark Blue |
| 6 | Red Brown | 17 | Light Green |
| 7 | Brown | 18 | Green |
| 8 | Dark Brown | 19 | Dark Green |
| 9 | Pink | 20 | Gray |
| 10 | Scarlet | 21 | Dark Gray |
| 11 | Red | 22 | Black |

| | | | | |
|---|---|---|---|---|
| 1 | Peach | 12 | Lilac |
| 2 | Yellow | 13 | Violet |
| 3 | Skin Tone | 14 | Light Blue |
| 4 | Orange | 15 | Blue |
| 5 | Orangered | 16 | Dark Blue |
| 6 | Red Brown | 17 | Light Green |
| 7 | Brown | 18 | Green |
| 8 | Dark Brown | 19 | Dark Green |
| 9 | Pink | 20 | Gray |
| 10 | Scarlet | 21 | Dark Gray |
| 11 | Red | 22 | Black |

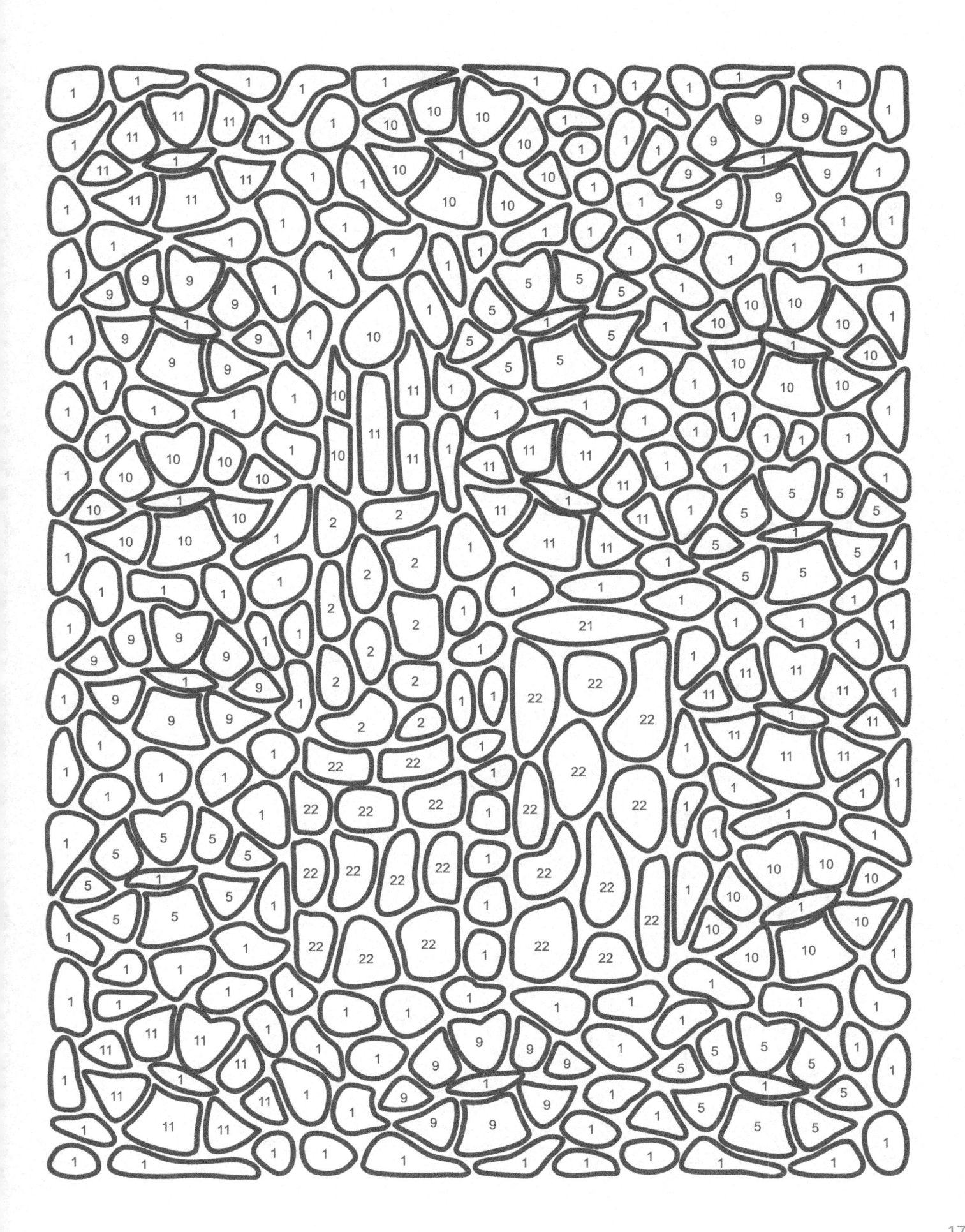

| | | | | |
|---|---|---|---|---|
| 1 | Peach | 12 | Lilac |
| 2 | Yellow | 13 | Violet |
| 3 | Skin Tone | 14 | Light Blue |
| 4 | Orange | 15 | Blue |
| 5 | Orangered | 16 | Dark Blue |
| 6 | Red Brown | 17 | Light Green |
| 7 | Brown | 18 | Green |
| 8 | Dark Brown | 19 | Dark Green |
| 9 | Pink | 20 | Gray |
| 10 | Scarlet | 21 | Dark Gray |
| 11 | Red | 22 | Black |

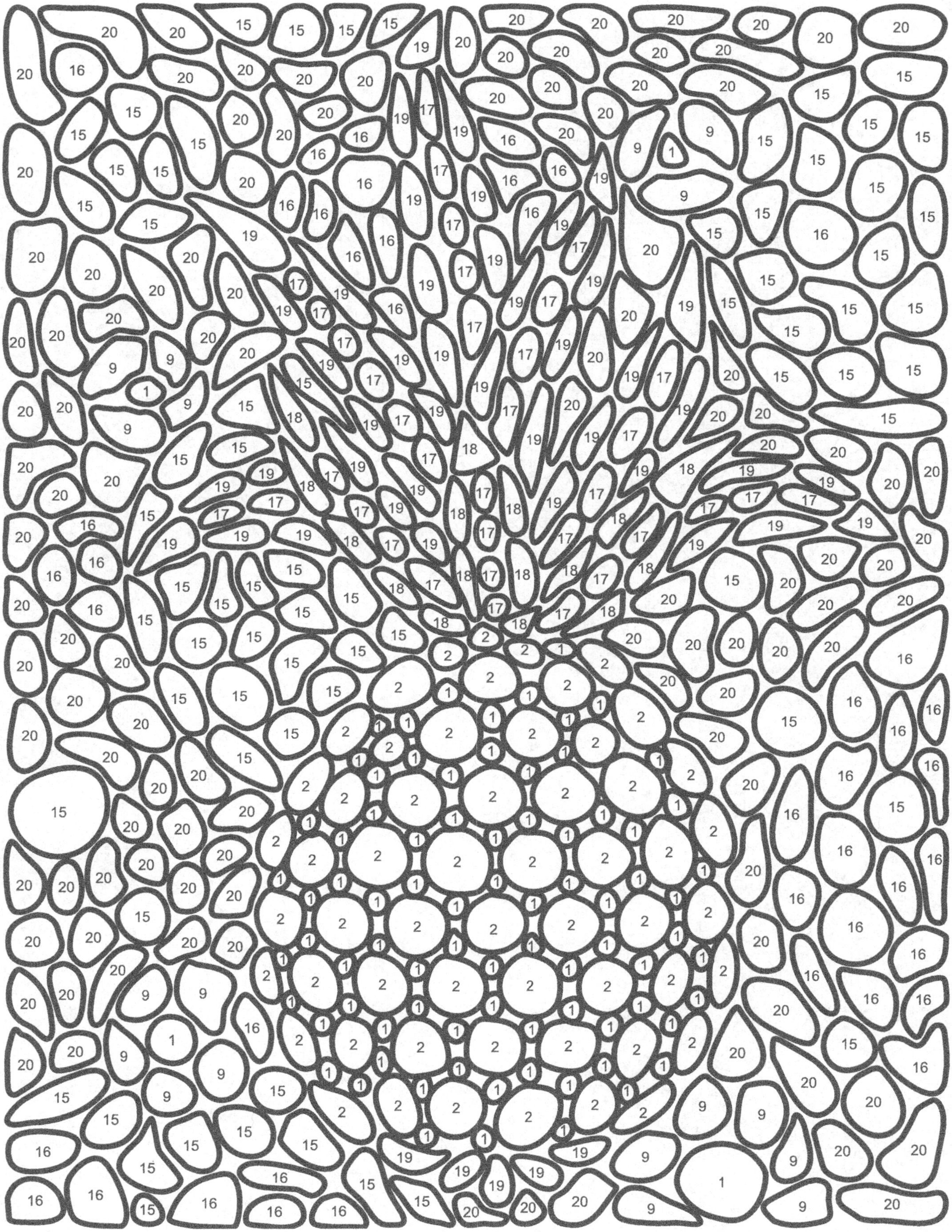

| | | | | |
|---|---|---|---|---|
| 1 | Peach | 12 | Lilac |
| 2 | Yellow | 13 | Violet |
| 3 | Skin Tone | 14 | Light Blue |
| 4 | Orange | 15 | Blue |
| 5 | Orangered | 16 | Dark Blue |
| 6 | Red Brown | 17 | Light Green |
| 7 | Brown | 18 | Green |
| 8 | Dark Brown | 19 | Dark Green |
| 9 | Pink | 20 | Gray |
| 10 | Scarlet | 21 | Dark Gray |
| 11 | Red | 22 | Black |

| | | | | |
|---|---|---|---|---|
| 1 | Peach | 12 | Lilac |
| 2 | Yellow | 13 | Violet |
| 3 | Skin Tone | 14 | Light Blue |
| 4 | Orange | 15 | Blue |
| 5 | Orangered | 16 | Dark Blue |
| 6 | Red Brown | 17 | Light Green |
| 7 | Brown | 18 | Green |
| 8 | Dark Brown | 19 | Dark Green |
| 9 | Pink | 20 | Gray |
| 10 | Scarlet | 21 | Dark Gray |
| 11 | Red | 22 | Black |

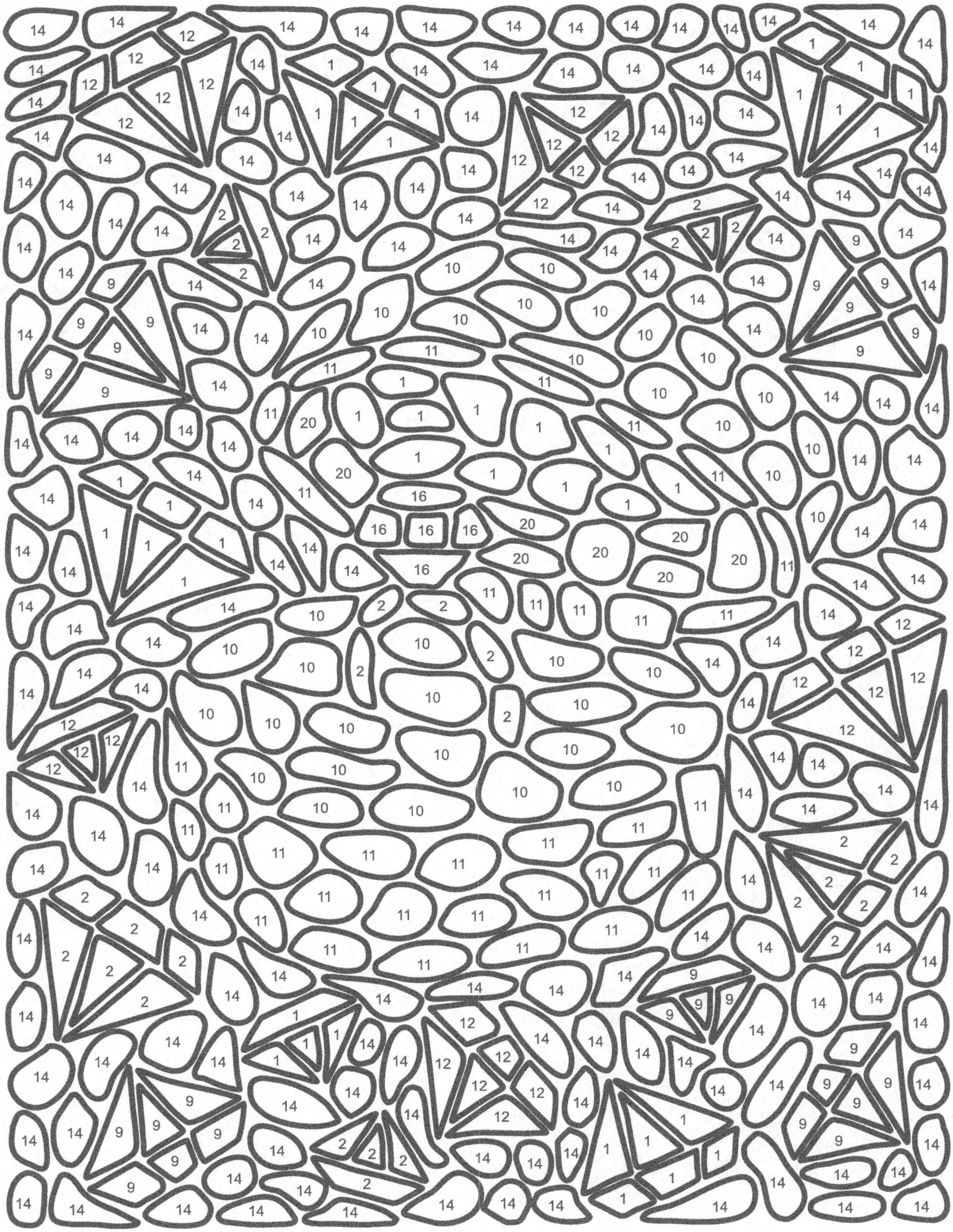

| | | | | |
|---|---|---|---|
| 1 | Peach | 12 | Lilac |
| 2 | Yellow | 13 | Violet |
| 3 | Skin Tone | 14 | Light Blue |
| 4 | Orange | 15 | Blue |
| 5 | Orangered | 16 | Dark Blue |
| 6 | Red Brown | 17 | Light Green |
| 7 | Brown | 18 | Green |
| 8 | Dark Brown | 19 | Dark Green |
| 9 | Pink | 20 | Gray |
| 10 | Scarlet | 21 | Dark Gray |
| 11 | Red | 22 | Black |

| | | | | | |
|---|---|---|---|---|---|
| 1 | Peach | 9 | Pink | 17 | Light Green |
| 2 | Yellow | 10 | Scarlet | 18 | Green |
| 3 | Skin Tone | 11 | Red | 19 | Dark Green |
| 4 | Orange | 12 | Lilac | 20 | Gray |
| 5 | Orangered | 13 | Violet | 21 | Dark Gray |
| 6 | Red Brown | 14 | Light Blue | 22 | Black |
| 7 | Brown | 15 | Blue | | |
| 8 | Dark Brown | 16 | Dark Blue | | |

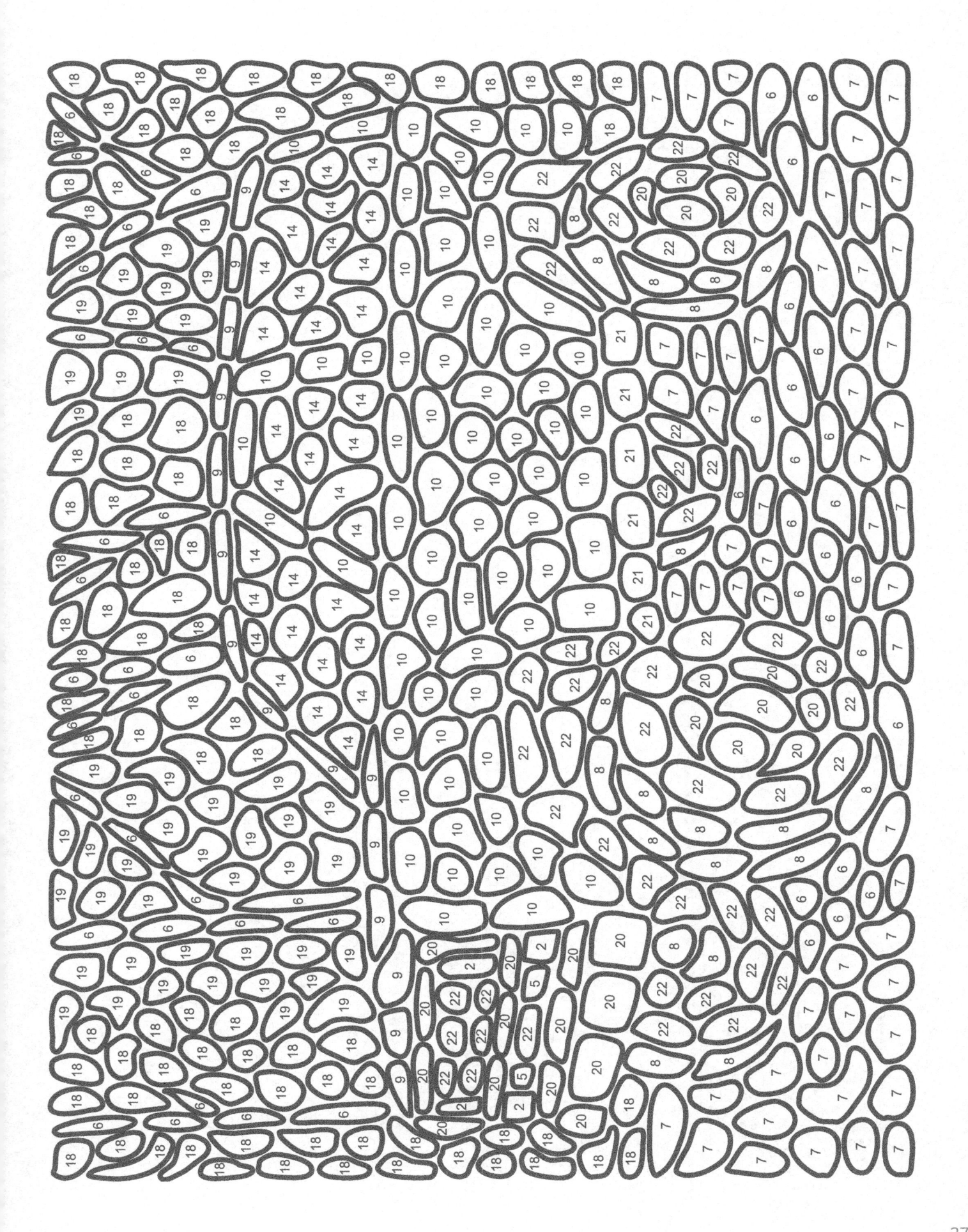

| | | | | | |
|---|---|---|---|---|---|
| 1 | Peach | 9 | Pink | 17 | Light Green |
| 2 | Yellow | 10 | Scarlet | 18 | Green |
| 3 | Skin Tone | 11 | Red | 19 | Dark Green |
| 4 | Orange | 12 | Lilac | 20 | Gray |
| 5 | Orangered | 13 | Violet | 21 | Dark Gray |
| 6 | Red Brown | 14 | Light Blue | 22 | Black |
| 7 | Brown | 15 | Blue | | |
| 8 | Dark Brown | 16 | Dark Blue | | |

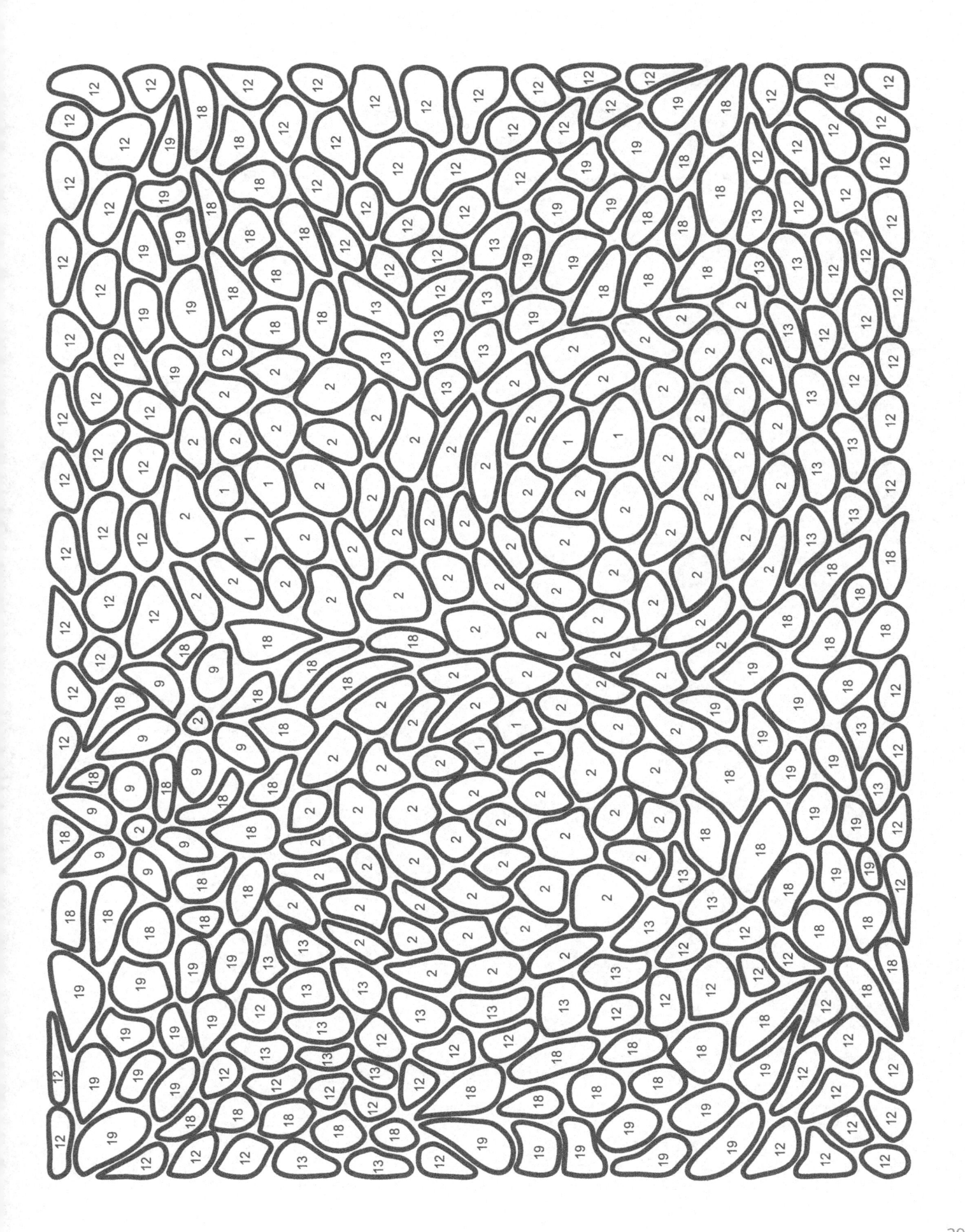

| | | | |
|---|---|---|---|
| 1 | Peach | 12 | Lilac |
| 2 | Yellow | 13 | Violet |
| 3 | Skin Tone | 14 | Light Blue |
| 4 | Orange | 15 | Blue |
| 5 | Orangered | 16 | Dark Blue |
| 6 | Red Brown | 17 | Light Green |
| 7 | Brown | 18 | Green |
| 8 | Dark Brown | 19 | Dark Green |
| 9 | Pink | 20 | Gray |
| 10 | Scarlet | 21 | Dark Gray |
| 11 | Red | 22 | Black |

| | | | | |
|---|---|---|---|---|
| 1 | Peach | 12 | Lilac |
| 2 | Yellow | 13 | Violet |
| 3 | Skin Tone | 14 | Light Blue |
| 4 | Orange | 15 | Blue |
| 5 | Orangered | 16 | Dark Blue |
| 6 | Red Brown | 17 | Light Green |
| 7 | Brown | 18 | Green |
| 8 | Dark Brown | 19 | Dark Green |
| 9 | Pink | 20 | Gray |
| 10 | Scarlet | 21 | Dark Gray |
| 11 | Red | 22 | Black |

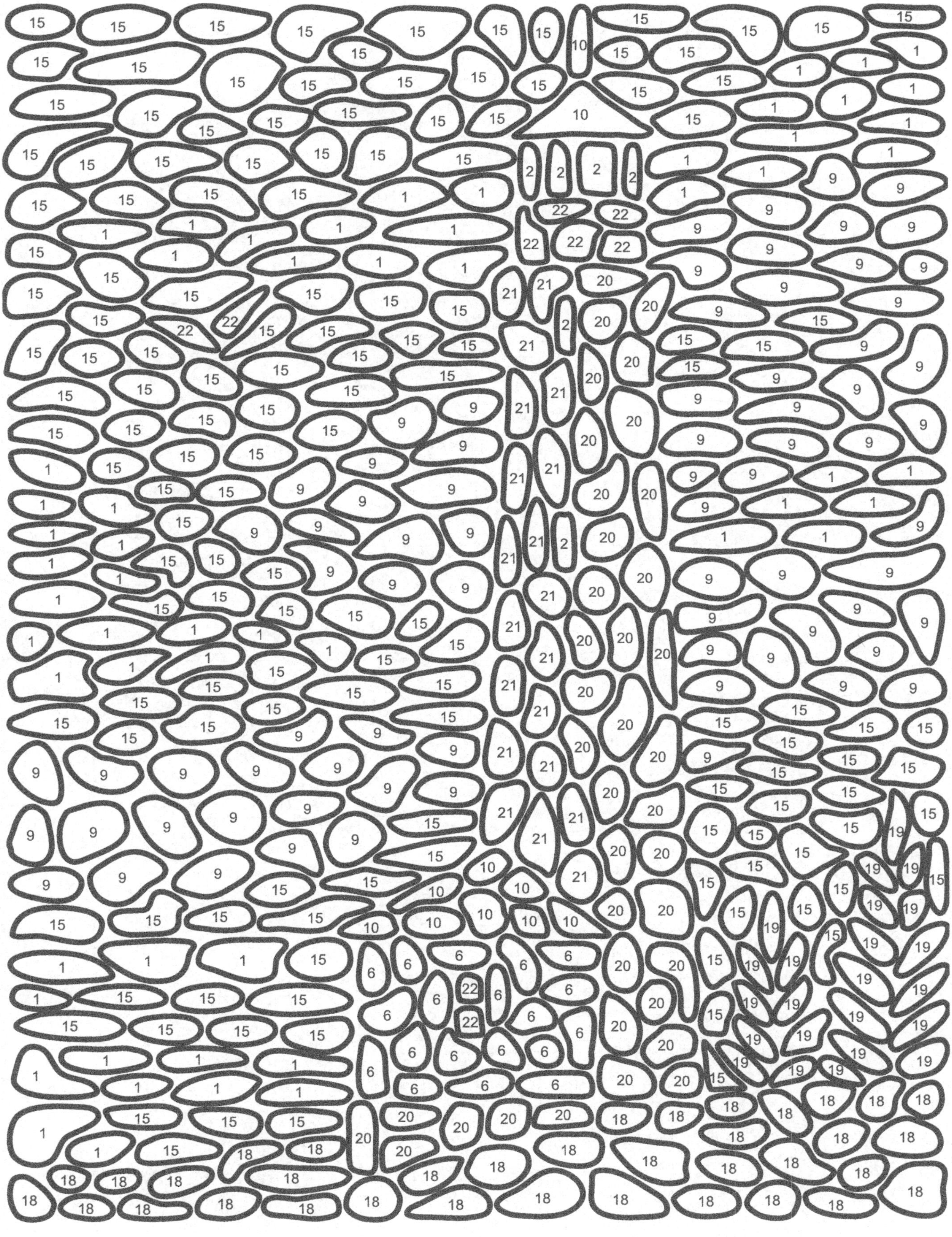

| | | | | |
|---|---|---|---|---|
| 1 | Peach | | 12 | Lilac |
| 2 | Yellow | | 13 | Violet |
| 3 | Skin Tone | | 14 | Light Blue |
| 4 | Orange | | 15 | Blue |
| 5 | Orangered | | 16 | Dark Blue |
| 6 | Red Brown | | 17 | Light Green |
| 7 | Brown | | 18 | Green |
| 8 | Dark Brown | | 19 | Dark Green |
| 9 | Pink | | 20 | Gray |
| 10 | Scarlet | | 21 | Dark Gray |
| 11 | Red | | 22 | Black |

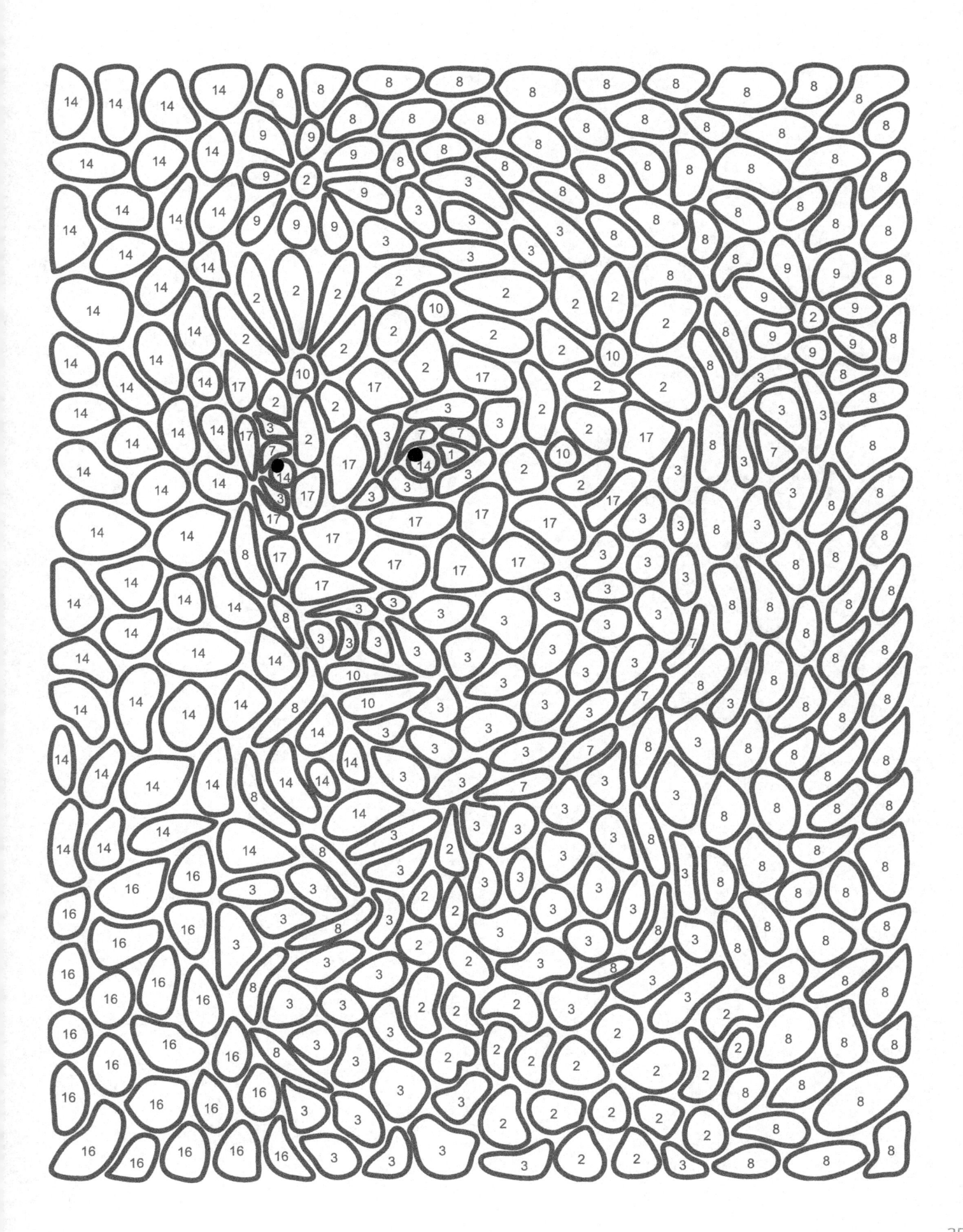

| 1 | Peach | 12 | Lilac |
|---|---|---|---|
| 2 | Yellow | 13 | Violet |
| 3 | Skin Tone | 14 | Light Blue |
| 4 | Orange | 15 | Blue |
| 5 | Orangered | 16 | Dark Blue |
| 6 | Red Brown | 17 | Light Green |
| 7 | Brown | 18 | Green |
| 8 | Dark Brown | 19 | Dark Green |
| 9 | Pink | 20 | Gray |
| 10 | Scarlet | 21 | Dark Gray |
| 11 | Red | 22 | Black |

| 1 | Peach | 9 | Pink | 17 | Light Green |
|---|---|---|---|---|---|
| 2 | Yellow | 10 | Scarlet | 18 | Green |
| 3 | Skin Tone | 11 | Red | 19 | Dark Green |
| 4 | Orange | 12 | Lilac | 20 | Gray |
| 5 | Orangered | 13 | Violet | 21 | Dark Gray |
| 6 | Red Brown | 14 | Light Blue | 22 | Black |
| 7 | Brown | 15 | Blue | | |
| 8 | Dark Brown | 16 | Dark Blue | | |

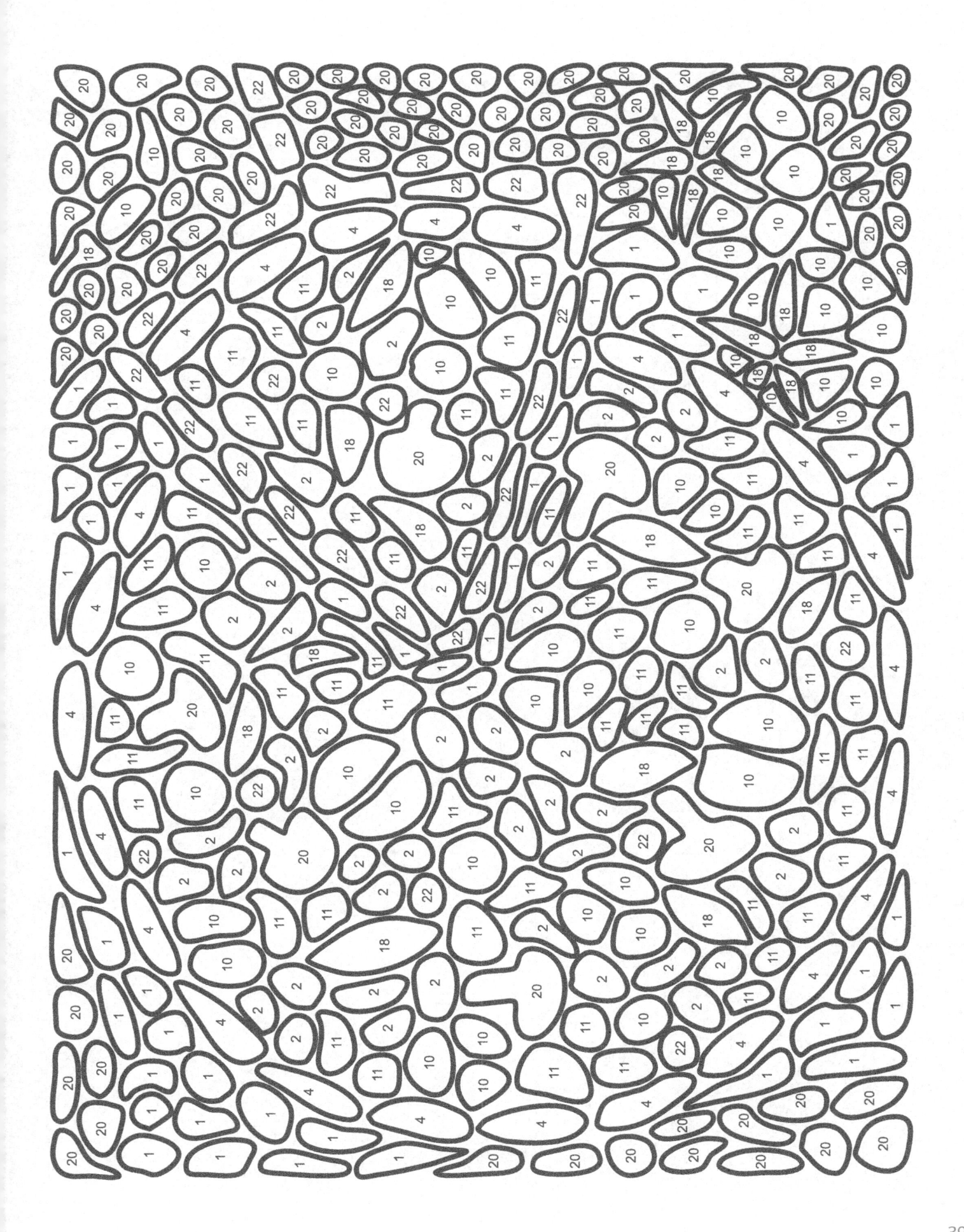

| | | | | |
|---|---|---|---|---|
| 1 | Peach | 12 | Lilac |
| 2 | Yellow | 13 | Violet |
| 3 | Skin Tone | 14 | Light Blue |
| 4 | Orange | 15 | Blue |
| 5 | Orangered | 16 | Dark Blue |
| 6 | Red Brown | 17 | Light Green |
| 7 | Brown | 18 | Green |
| 8 | Dark Brown | 19 | Dark Green |
| 9 | Pink | 20 | Gray |
| 10 | Scarlet | 21 | Dark Gray |
| 11 | Red | 22 | Black |

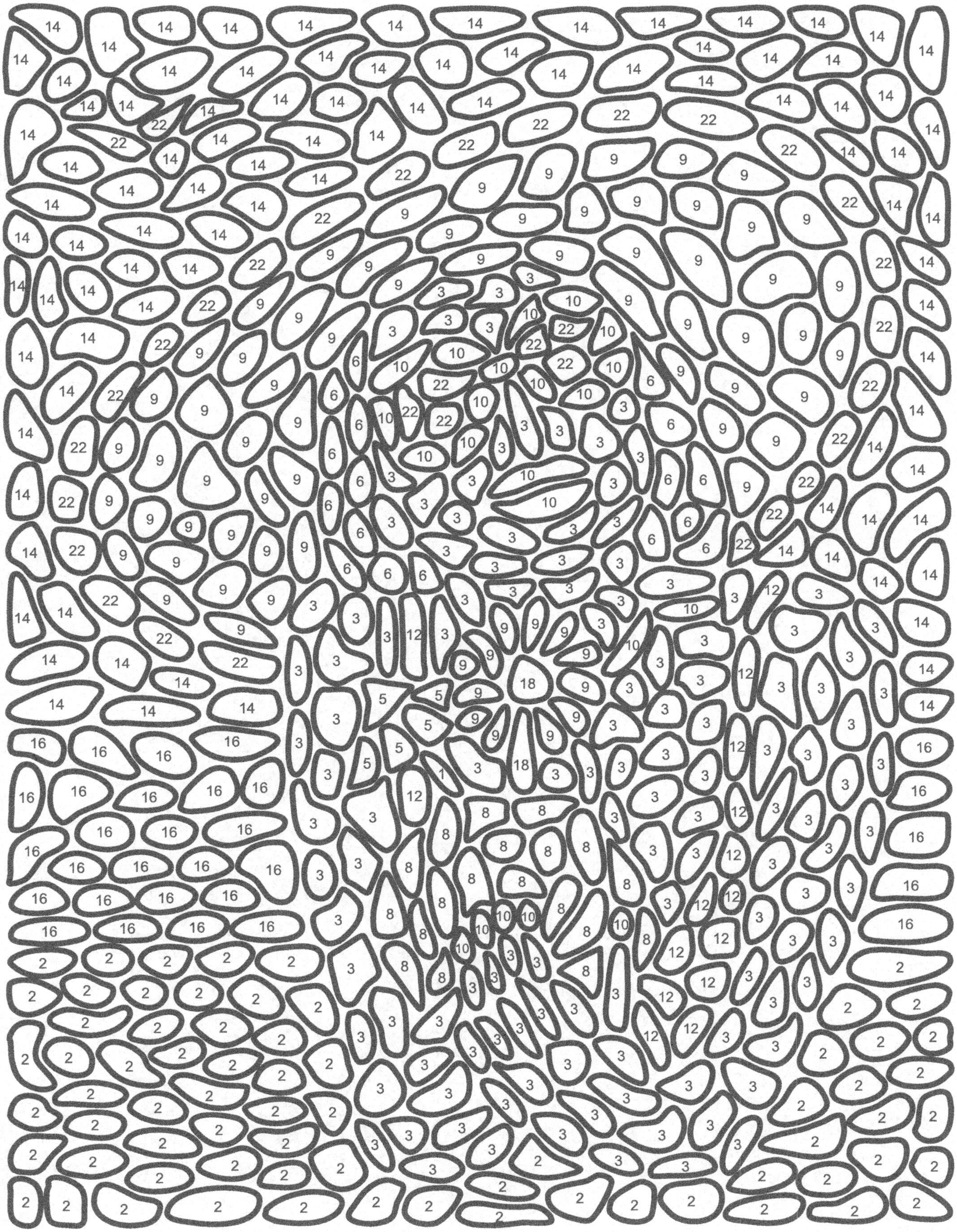

| 1 | Peach | 9 | Pink | 17 | Light Green |
|---|---|---|---|---|---|
| 2 | Yellow | 10 | Scarlet | 18 | Green |
| 3 | Skin Tone | 11 | Red | 19 | Dark Green |
| 4 | Orange | 12 | Lilac | 20 | Gray |
| 5 | Orangered | 13 | Violet | 21 | Dark Gray |
| 6 | Red Brown | 14 | Light Blue | 22 | Black |
| 7 | Brown | 15 | Blue | | |
| 8 | Dark Brown | 16 | Dark Blue | | |

| | | | |
|---|---|---|---|
| 1 | Peach | 12 | Lilac |
| 2 | Yellow | 13 | Violet |
| 3 | Skin Tone | 14 | Light Blue |
| 4 | Orange | 15 | Blue |
| 5 | Orangered | 16 | Dark Blue |
| 6 | Red Brown | 17 | Light Green |
| 7 | Brown | 18 | Green |
| 8 | Dark Brown | 19 | Dark Green |
| 9 | Pink | 20 | Gray |
| 10 | Scarlet | 21 | Dark Gray |
| 11 | Red | 22 | Black |

| | | | | |
|---|---|---|---|---|
| 1 | Peach | 12 | Lilac |
| 2 | Yellow | 13 | Violet |
| 3 | Skin Tone | 14 | Light Blue |
| 4 | Orange | 15 | Blue |
| 5 | Orangered | 16 | Dark Blue |
| 6 | Red Brown | 17 | Light Green |
| 7 | Brown | 18 | Green |
| 8 | Dark Brown | 19 | Dark Green |
| 9 | Pink | 20 | Gray |
| 10 | Scarlet | 21 | Dark Gray |
| 11 | Red | 22 | Black |

1 Peach
2 Yellow
3 Skin Tone
4 Orange
5 Orangered
6 Red Brown
7 Brown
8 Dark Brown

9 Pink
10 Scarlet
11 Red
12 Lilac
13 Violet
14 Light Blue
15 Blue
16 Dark Blue

17 Light Green
18 Green
19 Dark Green
20 Gray
21 Dark Gray
22 Black

49

1. Peach
2. Yellow
3. Skin Tone
4. Orange
5. Orangered
6. Red Brown
7. Brown
8. Dark Brown
9. Pink
10. Scarlet
11. Red
12. Lilac
13. Violet
14. Light Blue
15. Blue
16. Dark Blue
17. Light Green
18. Green
19. Dark Green
20. Gray
21. Dark Gray
22. Black

| | | | | | |
|---|---|---|---|---|---|
| 1 | Peach | 9 | Pink | 17 | Light Green |
| 2 | Yellow | 10 | Scarlet | 18 | Green |
| 3 | Skin Tone | 11 | Red | 19 | Dark Green |
| 4 | Orange | 12 | Lilac | 20 | Gray |
| 5 | Orangered | 13 | Violet | 21 | Dark Gray |
| 6 | Red Brown | 14 | Light Blue | 22 | Black |
| 7 | Brown | 15 | Blue | | |
| 8 | Dark Brown | 16 | Dark Blue | | |

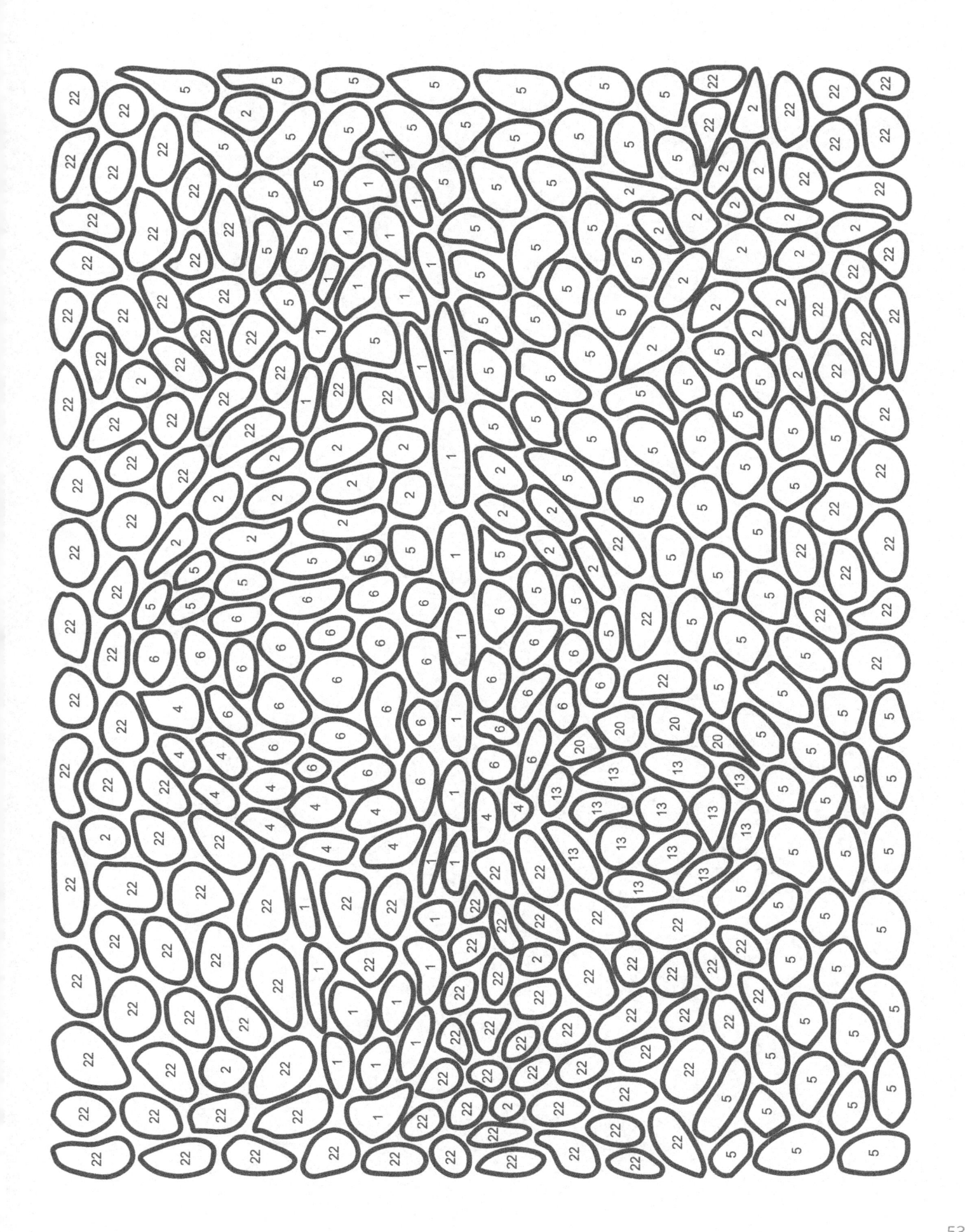

| | | | |
|---|---|---|---|
| 1 | Peach | 12 | Lilac |
| 2 | Yellow | 13 | Violet |
| 3 | Skin Tone | 14 | Light Blue |
| 4 | Orange | 15 | Blue |
| 5 | Orangered | 16 | Dark Blue |
| 6 | Red Brown | 17 | Light Green |
| 7 | Brown | 18 | Green |
| 8 | Dark Brown | 19 | Dark Green |
| 9 | Pink | 20 | Gray |
| 10 | Scarlet | 21 | Dark Gray |
| 11 | Red | 22 | Black |

# WE ARE THE BELBA FAMILY.

Thank you for your choice.

All books are made with love for People and Nature.

We appreciate your feedback with a small review of the book on Amazon, Facebook, or Instagram.

If you tag your colored pages as #belbafamily, we share your work on our social media pages.

You help us to make our books better.

**Stay safe and happy coloring!**

Follow us:

f  https://www.facebook.com/belbafamily/

⊙  Belba Family

𝕏  @BelbaFamily

You and your artworks inspired us to open the Belba Family Shop, where you can find different merch with best designs from our books!

⊙  Belba Family Shop

🛒  BELBA.redbubble.com

# TRY THE OTHER BOOK SERIES BY THE BELBA FAMILY:

**The MOSAIC color by number ART activity book series includes:**

- TRAVEL MOSAIC. Color by Number ART activity book.
- ANIMAL MOSAIC. Color by number ART activity book.

**Color by number & coloring version books:**

- CHRISTMAS & TRAVEL MOSAICS. An adult book with relaxing pages of Christmas scenes around the world.
- THE MONEY BOOK. An adult magic book with Money & Richness symbols to color.
- FAIRIES AROUND US. Stained Glass & Magic Mosaics. An adult Book for relaxation and stress relief.

**PUZZLE COLOR BY NUMBER CLEVER BOOK SERIES:**

BEGINNER level
(no background):

- SIMPLE BEAUTY
- HUMAN FACES

ADVANCED level
(with background):

- EXOTIC LIFE
- SECRET PATTERNS

**STONE MOSAIC SERIES:**

- BOOK 1
- BOOK 2
- BOOK 3

**3 COLORS SERIES:**

- CELEBRITIES
- ANIMALS & BIRDS

**MYSTERY MOSAICS books series with 3*3 mm. sections:**

- MYSTERY MOSAICS. PASSION
- MYSTERY MOSAICS. DOGS
- MYSTERY MOSAICS. WOMAN
- SQUARE MANDALAS (Book 1)
- MYSTERY MOSAICS. GALLERY
- MYSTERY MOSAICS. WOW, CATS!
- SQUARE MANDALAS. ANIMALS IN PATTERNS (Book 2)
- MYSTERY MOSAICS. CINEMA
- LISA'S GARDEN. SQUARE MANDALAS, PATTERNS, AND MORE
- MYSTERY MOSAICS. WOW, ANIMALS!
- MYSTERY MOSAICS. FLOWERS
- MYSTERY MOSAICS. ARIANE'S VINTAGE COLLECTION
- PARTY PATTERNS
- ALL ABOUT CHRISTMAS
- SQUARE MANDALAS (Book 3)
- MYSTERY MOSAICS. SECRET PATTERNS
- MYSTERY MOSAICS. WOW, AFRICA!

And more...

**HAPPY COLORING!**

Made in the USA
Las Vegas, NV
30 June 2021